IM.POSSIBLE

BUILDING RESILIENT STUDENTS
WHO CHASE THEIR DREAMS

INCLUDES WORKSHEETS BASED ON THE IM.POSSIBLE SCHOOL ASSEMBLY

EDDIE CORTES

CONTENTS

INTRODUCTION

Have you ever had a dream that was so big, so awesome, so epic that it felt impossible to achieve?

Sometimes your dreams feel like they are out of reach, like they're impossible to obtain. This could be because of internal struggles. Maybe because you feel like you are not good enough or you are afraid to fail. There may be other external obstacles, your life circumstances or limitations that seem impossible to overcome; it feels like the odds are not in your favor.

For some of you the obstacles may be larger and tougher; nevertheless I'm convinced that it is not your obstacles, circumstances, limitations, but your determined effort that drives you towards your desired destination in life.

In other words, your willpower, your grit, your resilience will ultimately determine whether you chase your dreams or not.

This book is a tool I have created to empower you by teaching you how to build resilience.

ABOUT RESILIENCE

Resilience is a fancy word for the ability to bounce back from hard things to accomplish hard things. It is a skill you can grow as you respond to adversity. Adversity is any challenge that you face, which can be anything from stress, failure, and trauma. The challenges can be anything from moving away from a community and losing friends to dealing with divorce and balancing the tension of broken relationships. These challenges can be incredibly difficult to overcome but not impossible; resilience <u>can be</u> learned.

IMPOSSIBLE VS IM.POSSIBLE

The word "impossible" can be broken down into the two words "im" and "possible." This suggests that even though something may seem impossible at first, there may be a way to approach it that makes it achievable. In other words, something that is considered impossible may not be completely out of reach. With resilience, the right attitude, and approach, it may be possible to overcome any obstacles and achieve your dream.

MY MISSION

It is my mission to empower students like you to rise above your circumstances and accomplish your dreams. My goal is to help you to realize that you are not defined by your limitations, your failure, your circumstances, but instead your potential lies within your response to the obstacles and your endurance as you overcome each one. I want you to discover that you are brave, strong, smart, and capable of realizing your dreams are possible.

Now, let's learn how to chase that im.**possible** dream.

CHAPTER 1

IMPOSSIBLE DREAM

"Nothing is impossible, the word itself says 'I'm possible'!"

— Audrey Hepburn

"Welcome folks! If you are just tuning in, we are in the bottom of the 9th of Game 7 of the American League Championship. The game is tied, the bases are loaded, and there are two outs. MVP candidate Eddie Cortes is up to bat," says the baseball announcer as he leans into the microphone.

"Listen to that crowd. Boy, are they cheering loudly! Yankee fans are really hoping Eddie brings home the win."

"Eddie steps into the batter's box."

"The pitcher stares him down, he winds up, sets, and throws a fastball high and away."

"Eddie swings with everything that he has and misses big."

"STRIKE," yells the umpire, as he holds up the 0 and 1 sign.

The crowd lets out a huge groan and the cheers become faint.

The announcer continues, "Eddie steps out of the batter's box and takes a deep breath. He is 2 for 3 today with an RBI double."

The cheers and chants begin to ramp up again, growing louder and louder.

The announcer's voice ominous as he begins again. Eddie steps in the batter's box. The count against him with 1 strike. The game is tied. We're in the bottom of the 9th and the bases are loaded. He needs a hit here to break the tie and bring a runner home for the win.

The pitcher nods at his call, stares down the batter, winds up, sets, and here's the pitch. Curveball down and away, strike 2, screams the umpire with great excitement.

The umpire holds up the 0-2 sign. The announcer explains, "he tried checking his bat, but the swing was too late."

"Eddie really looked in trouble with that curve ball."

"He steps out of the batter's box and takes a few practice swings."

The cheers elevate, the volume the loudest it has been. The tension and excitement at its peak.

"Eddie steps in the batter's box. The bases are loaded. Derek Jeter is on third. He's the winning run. Two outs. It'll be an 0-2 pitch."

"Eddie is staring the pitcher down as he sweeps a little

dirt away from the left side of the pitcher's stand. The pitcher tugs once at the bill of his cap, takes a deep breath, winds up, and the pitch. It is a fastball right down the plate. Eddie swings, connecting with the ball. Strongly hit, it is high in the air, deep to center field."

The crowd erupts in a deafening cheer.

"The center fielder runs back, way back, he's on the track, at the wall, it is..."

No, I did not hit the game winning home run though that would have been an epic ending to an epic dream. Instead, this dream ended with a tennis ball crashing through the living room window.

See, I was just a kid, in my living room, with a tennis ball and wiffle bat, dreaming of playing in the American League Championship for the New York Yankees in front of the home crowd.

My mother, hearing the glass shatter, yelled, "Heriiiiiiiiiiiberto Cortes Acevedo Cruz Soto, what did you break now?" She storms into the living room with her chancleta (flip flop) raised in her hand. I take one look at her, and take off running to hide in my bedroom and slide into my closet.

SAFE!

Playing baseball for the New York Yankees, that was my dream. That was my impossible dream.

What's yours?

DISCUSSION QUESTIONS

1. What was the author's dream as a child?
2. What was the situation in the baseball game described in the chapter?
3. How did the crowd react to Eddie's last at-bat?
4. What happened at the end of the dream?
5. Why did the dream end with a broken window?

WHAT'S YOUR IMPOSSIBLE DREAM?

_____

Write down your impossible dream here.

IF YOU CAN DREAM IT, YOU CAN ACHIEVE IT.

ZIG ZIGLAR

▶ NOTES

*"THE ONLY WAY TO DO THE IMPOSSIBLE IS TO
BELIEVE IT IS POSSIBLE."*

CHARLES KINGSLEIGH

DISCOVERING MY
IM.POSSIBLE DREAM

What am I good at?

I'm interested in:

What do I love to do?

I'd like to learn more about:

What do I care about most?

What makes me happy?

CHAPTER 2

DO HARD THINGS

I can bounce back from adversity and reinvent my life – it's possible.

— Les Brown

Chasing your impossible dream will take resilience. This book will dare you to continue to dream; while empowering you to challenge yourself to do hard things, face failure, and overcome obstacles. Dreams become your reality when you bounce back from challenges to achieve things you never thought were possible.

Failure to make the drama club is hard. Dealing with your parents' divorce is difficult. Struggling through money troubles is challenging. Not feeling accepted by your peers is frustrating. Instead of feeling defeated, as these difficulties arise, resilience drives you to face those hard things with a good attitude and move forward with a hopeful outlook.

Re·sil·ience
(rə'zilēəns)

The ability to bounce back
from hard things to do hard things.

EMILY'S STORY

Emily had a major stuttering problem in grade school. It was so bad that she could barely hold a conversation with her classmates. Emily was smart, she had a lot to say, but had a hard time speaking.

In junior high, a teacher encouraged her to try out for the school play. Emily had no interest, if her stutter made it difficult to talk with friends, she felt it would be impossible to speak on stage in front of an audience. But her teacher did not relent, he challenged Emily to face her stuttering problem. And that's exactly what she did.

Emily found the courage to try out for the school play. At first, it was not easy to read the script out loud, her stutter would often get the best of her. One day the

teacher suggested that Emily say her lines in funny voices or accents to try to minimize the stuttering–and it worked! By the time she graduated high school, Emily overcame her stutter and was speaking fluently.

Instead of feeling defeated by her impediment, Emily decided to do hard things to chase her dream. It took courage, creativity, and commitment; it took a resilient effort to bounce back from an "impossible" stutter to act in her school play. She could barely imagine making her school play at first, let alone a career in film.

Today Emily Blunt is a British actress and recipient of the Golden Globe Award for best supporting actress. You can watch Emily star in movies like Disney's The Jungle Cruise and Mary Poppins Returns.

CAN-DO

You too, can do hard things. In fact, as you chase your impossible dream you will face obstacles, challenges, and adversity. Developing the skill of resilience will help you...

adapt to changes,
strengthen your mind,
expect failure and use them as learning opportunities,
make decisions that are tough with confidence,
bounce back from adversity,
and chase your im.possible dream.

BOUNCE BACK

Professor Helen McGrath has an acronym from her resiliency program for principles that will help you cope with hard things and develop the skill to bounce back.

Bad times don't last, and things get better.

Other people can only help if you share with them.

Unhelpful thinking only makes you feel worse.

Nobody is perfect – not you, not your friends, not your family, not anybody!

Concentrate on the good things in life, no matter how small.

Everybody suffers, everybody feels pain and experiences setbacks; they are a normal part of life.

Blame fairly – negative events are often a combination of things you did, things others did, and plain bad luck.

Accept what you can't change and try to change what you can.

Catastrophizing makes things worse – don't fall prey to believing in the worst interpretation.

Keep things in perspective. Even the worst moment is but one moment in life.

Chasing your im.possible dream will take resilience. As you encounter situations that are difficult, maintain a good attitude, and move forward with a hopeful outlook, to bounce back. With this perspective you will do things you never thought were possible. Just like Emily Blunt.

DISCUSSION QUESTIONS

1. What is resilience and why is it important to chase your dreams?
2. How did Emily Blunt develop resilience to overcome her stuttering problem?
3. What are some of the benefits of developing resilience in the face of adversity?
4. How can you develop the skill of resilience to do hard things?
5. What are some of the principles for coping with hard things and bouncing back from setbacks, according to Professor Helen McGrath's resiliency program?

DO NOT JUDGE ME BY MY SUCCESS, JUDGE ME BY HOW MANY TIMES I FELL DOWN AND GOT BACK UP AGAIN.

NELSON MANDELA

▶ NOTES

DO HARD THINGS

Describe an obstacle you recently encountered.

How can you face this obstacle with a better more positive attitude?

Who could you share this with that can help?

What would you say to encourage a friend facing the same obstacle?

CHAPTER 3

PEOPLE DO IM.POSSIBLE THINGS

*"I hope you all know that nothing can stop you.
If you can be tough, if you can be creative, if you
can believe in who you are and what you
can do, nothing in this world can
hold you back."*

— Jim Abbott

Tazio Gavioli from Italy can do twenty-three consecutive pinky pull ups. If it was not in the Guinness Book of World Records, I would have said, impossible! Most adults can not do three regular pull ups consecutively let alone pinky pull ups.

Takeru Kobayashi ate twelve hamburgers in three minutes. Unbelievable. I got full eating a double cheeseburger last week.

And Fergal "Eyesore" Fleming can go nearly forty-two minutes without blinking. Awesome, right! How long can you go? Do you think you could read the rest of this chapter without blinking?

To me, Jim Abbott's story is even more impressive than those awesome feats.

Jim's childhood dream was to play Major League Baseball despite being born without a right hand. The odds of playing in the big leagues are stacked against even the most talented baseball players. For perspective, you are more likely to get struck by lightning than you are to play in the Major Leagues. For someone with one hand, the odds seemed virtually impossible.

Historically baseball was a two-handed sport. You bat with two hands, which helps to keep the bat steady and balanced. You also need two hands to generate enough bat speed to hit the ball.

Players also use one hand to catch the ball and the other hand to throw the ball. Having only one hand seems to

make playing baseball impossible.

Jim Abbott did not let having only one hand stop him from chasing his dream. In fact, he embraced the challenge in creative ways. With his father's help, Jim learned to switch his glove on and off to catch and throw the baseball with the same hand.

Jim practiced by throwing a rubber ball against a wall and catching it on the rebound. At first, he missed often but never gave up even when his many failures were discouraging. Every time Jim failed to catch the rubber ball, he learned something new and tried again, and again, and again. As Jim improved, he challenged himself further by moving closer to the wall, developing a faster glove-hand switch. Jim, determined to chase his dream, saw the odds simply as an opportunity to accomplish the impossible.

The physical challenges were hard to overcome, but Jim Abbott also had to endure many mental and emotional challenges as he pursued his goal. One of the most significant challenges Jim faced was overcoming his doubters, those who could not and would not accept his dream could become a reality.

Jim frequently heard comments like:

"You will never play baseball, you only have one hand."

"There is no way you can catch and throw a baseball with one hand, especially as good as everyone else."

"You cannot bat with one hand."

"You will never play baseball at the highest level."

Jim Abbott tuned out the doubters, overcame his obstacles, and did the impossible. At eleven years old, he was the star player of his team. In high school, Jim was an outstanding pitcher and posted an incredible .427 career batting average. In college, he led the University of Michigan to two Big Ten Conference championships. During his junior year, Jim pitched the U.S. Olympic team to victory over Japan winning an unofficial gold medal. And in 1989 Jim Abbott fulfilled his im.possible dream of playing Major League Baseball as a member of the California Angels.

To say Jim's story is remarkable is an understatement. What he has accomplished up to this point is nothing short of awesome. But what he did next is even more incredible.

On September 4, 1993, as a member of the New York Yankees, Jim pitched a no-hitter against the Cleveland Guardians (formerly known as Indians). Which means he pitched the whole game without allowing a single hit. As of this writing, there have been 318 no-hitters, Jim is the only pitcher on this elite list to have done so with one hand.

Now that is phenomenal!

Jim Abbott's determination to overcome his obstacles is not just a sports thing, but a life thing. In addition to learning how to play baseball, Jim had to figure out how to do everyday things with one hand. Things like putting toothpaste on his toothbrush, buttoning up his shirt, and tying his shoelaces. What makes him special is not just that he pitched a no-hitter in a Major League Baseball game with one hand, it's that he overcame everyday obstacles in order to do so.

If Jim Abbott did these hard things, imagine what you can do?

Here are a few things I learned from Jim Abbott's story:

- You must do hard things to chase your dream.

- You can do hard things with a positive attitude and hard work.

- You will fail from time to time, but that is okay, because failures teach you how to succeed. The truth is you only really fail when you stop trying.

- You may have people doubt your dreams and tell you that it cannot be one.

- You may need help along the way from people to teach you how to do hard things.

People like Emily, Tazio, Takeru, Fergal, and Jim have done amazing and awe-inspiring feats which many thought to be impossible. They all were ordinary people with extraordinary dreams and the determination to pursue their im.possible dream. Whether it is starring in a movie, doing pinky pull-ups, eating a dozen hamburgers, going a few minutes without blinking, throwing a no-hitter, or by simply chasing an impossible dream.

Now it's your turn, go chase the im.possible.

DISCUSSION QUESTIONS

1. What is Jim Abbott's story and why is it remarkable?
2. How did Jim Abbott learn to overcome the physical challenges of playing baseball with one hand?
3. What mental and emotional challenges did Jim Abbott have to overcome to pursue his dream of playing baseball in the Major Leagues?
4. What lessons can you learn from Jim Abbott's story about achieving your dreams and goals?
5. What are some other examples of people who have achieved im.possible things, and what can we learn from them?

THERE WILL BE OBSTACLES. THERE WILL BE DOUBTERS. THERE WILL BE MISTAKES. BUT WITH HARD WORK, THERE ARE NO LIMITS.

MICHAEL PHELPS

NOTES

"YOU AREN'T BOUND BY THE CIRCUMSTANCES IN WHICH YOU WERE BORN.
YOU AREN'T BOUND BY THE SITUATION THAT YOU MIGHT FIND YOURSELF
IN AT THIS PARTICULAR MOMENT. I KNOW YOU ARE GOING TO GO
THROUGH DIFFICULT TIMES, BUT BELIEVE ME, IF YOU ARE
OPTIMISTIC AND HAVE GOOD PEOPLE AROUND YOU,
AND BELIEVE IN WHAT'S POSSIBLE, SO MANY GOOD
THINGS CAN HAPPEN IN THIS WORLD."

JIM ABBOTT

FAILING FORWARD

Reflect on a difficult activity and answer
the following questions.

Difficult activity:

What did you do well?

What did not go well?

What could you do differently next time?

CHAPTER 4

WORTHY OF YOUR DREAM

"You are enough not because you did or said or thought or bought or became or created something special, but because you always were."

– Marisa Peer

During my middle school years, I dreamed of playing professional baseball for my favorite team, the New York Yankees. They were my favorite team. Don Mattingly, who is my favorite player, played for them at the time. He was one of the best players in the league and the team captain. I was such a fan that I collected hundreds and hundreds of his baseball cards, and I dreamed of playing baseball for the Yankees like Don Mattingly.

One day my cousin and I watched a Yankees game on TV. It was a fun, exciting, and gut-wrenching baseball game.

The Yankees had hit a few doubles and a home run in the first inning to take the lead. They were winning. My cousin was giggling, I was happy, and were all smiling.

A couple innings later the Yankees lost the lead. Now the game is tied. The mood changed, I was no longer happy and there were no more laughs.

By the fifth inning the Yankees were losing by five runs. My cousin and I were no longer smiling.

However in the 6th inning the Yankees scored a run. In the seventh and eighth innings they scored again. The Yankees are making a comeback which brought my cousin to the edge of the sofa. I stood in front of the TV hoping, praying the Yankees pull out a win.

In the bottom of the ninth inning, the Yankees had runners on second and third base and my favorite player had come to bat with a chance to win the game. On the first pitch, Don Mattingly hit the game winning three-run home run.

The excitement in the room was bonkers, my cousin had begun jumping up and down on the sofa. I too joined in the celebration as we screamed, "the Yankees win, the Yankees win, the Yankees win!"

From the kitchen mom heard all the commotion and yelled, "Eddie, you better not break another window."

"Boys, go outside and play."

As we grabbed our baseball gear and headed towards the park we chatted about our favorite highlights of the game.

Mattingly's heroics had inspired me so much that I mustered up the courage to tell my cousin about my im.possible dream. I shared with him that I was going to play baseball, become a Yankee, and team captain just like Mattingly. I also told him that one day I was going to play in the American League Championship and hit the game winning homerun.

He suddenly stopped walking, looked me dead in the eyes, slowly smiled, and started laughing at me. It was a

wicked laugh. Then he said three words, "You? That's impossible!"

I vividly remember my excitement fading away. His laughter and disbelief still haunt me today.

He continued in his doubt to point out all my limitations, saying, "Dude, you will never play for the Yankees. You are not big enough, or strong enough, or fast enough to play in the big leagues. Eddie, you will never be good enough to play baseball for the New York Yankees."

I was devastated, my confidence was shaken, and my dream crushed.

Up to that point, I never thought about being good enough. I just believed I could do it. Impossible or not, that was my dream but from that day forward I struggled with not being enough.

My cousin's doubt made me stop believing in myself.

This experience may seem insignificant to most people but let me assure you, it had a negative impact on how I viewed myself for several years, even as I became an adult. The old adage, "sticks and stones may break my bones, but words will never hurt me," is completely untrue. Words hurt.

I was an impressionable middle schooler, my belief in

myself was vulnerable, especially from the doubt of my older cousin whom I had looked up to all my life. His words carried more weight than even the banter of my closest friends. And since I did not know how to cope with his negative words and doubt, I stopped believing in myself. I also stopped chasing my dream. It now became impossible.

Have you ever had someone crush your confidence? Have you felt that you are not enough? Have you stopped believing in yourself?

Unfortunately, many of us have experienced these feelings and have had doubts develop.

I want you to know and realize that YOU ARE ENOUGH!

"You are braver than you believe, stronger than you seem, and smarter than you think." In other words, you are worthy of your dream.

My experience taught me two things.

First, I realized that my self-worth is not determined by how big, strong, or fast I am. Nor is it determined by what my cousin (or anyone else) thinks of my talent. In fact, the truth is that I am loveable, significant, and of incomprehensible worth whether I'm good enough to play the game of baseball or not.

Are you ready for this fact, SO ARE YOU.

Your self-worth and ability to achieve your goals is not determined by your physical attributes, intelligence, friends, or family. Your self-worth is not changed by how good you are at something. Nor is it determined by what your peers think of you. The fact is you are loveable, significant, and of incomprehensible worth, as you are right now.

Secondly, I learned to never give up on myself. I didn't just give up on my dream, I stopped believing in myself. When you stop believing, you also stop dreaming. Truth is I am not a professional baseball player because I gave up on myself before I worked on building my skills and seeing if I could be good enough to play in the big leagues.

For dreams to come true, it takes a lot of work, but the

most important aspect to pursue and accomplish your dream is believing in yourself. You hold this power in your hands entirely. Don't ever give up on yourself as you chase your dreams. You are worthy of achieving your dream, even the impossible ones.

A belief in yourself, in who you are, is what turns the impossible dream into the achievable im.possible reality. Believe. You are worthy of your dream, IM.POSSIBLE.

DISCUSSION QUESTIONS

1. What did the author dream of during his middle school years and for which team?

2. What was the mood during the Yankees game that the author and his cousin watched on TV?

3. Who is the author's favorite player and what did he do to win the game?

4. How did the author's cousin respond when the author shared his dream of playing baseball for the Yankees?

5. What two things did the author learn from his experience of having his confidence crushed and his dream crushed by his cousin's doubt?

BELIEVE.
YOU ARE
WORTHY
OF YOUR
DREAM.

EDDIE CORTES

 # NOTES

"YOU ALONE ARE ENOUGH. YOU HAVE NOTHING TO PROVE TO ANYONE."

MAYA ANGELOU

ABOUT ME

I was really happy when...

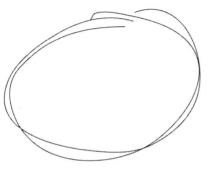

I'm proud of...

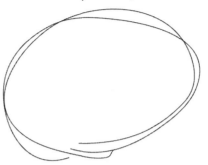

My family was happy when I...

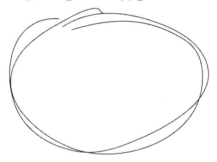

In school, I'm good at...

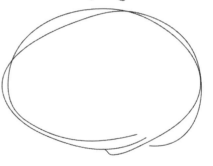

Something that makes me unique is...

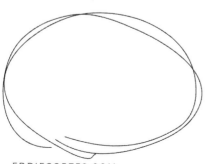

Something that my friends like about me is...

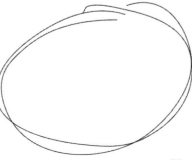

NOTES

"YOUR SELF-WORTH IS DETERMINED BY YOU. YOU DON'T HAVE TO DEPEND ON SOMEONE TELLING YOU WHO YOU ARE."

BEYONCÉ

I AM ENOUGH

Based on how you feel, rate the following statements from **1** to **5**. **1** means you don't believe it at all, and **5** means you completely believe it.

STATEMENTS

RATING

1. I believe in myself. ① ② ③ ④ ⑤
2. I'm just as valuable as other people. ① ② ③ ④ ⑤
3. I am proud of my accomplishments. ① ② ③ ④ ⑤
4. I would rather be me than someone else. ① ② ③ ④ ⑤
5. I feel good when I get compliments. ① ② ③ ④ ⑤
6. I can handle criticism. ① ② ③ ④ ⑤
7. I focus on my success and not my failures. ① ② ③ ④ ⑤
8. I love myself even when others reject me. ① ② ③ ④ ⑤
9. I know my positive qualities. ① ② ③ ④ ⑤
10. I am not afraid to make mistakes. ① ② ③ ④ ⑤

Add up all your ratings and divide the total by **10** to get your score. **1** means your struggling with your self-worth and **5** means you are not.

① ② ③ ④ ⑤

I am enough and I am worthy of my dream.

Write on the line below what needs to change to grow your overall self-worth by just one point?

_____

_____

CHAPTER 5

WORDS MATTER

Words matter. And the words that matter most are the ones you say to yourself.

– David Taylor-Klaus

"I cannot."

"There's no way I can do that."

"I'm just not brave enough."

Have you ever had those thoughts or thoughts like these?

Those were the negative thoughts that my inner critic (the little voice in my head) was screaming at me as I got ready to rappel down an eight-thousand-foot mountain in Utah.

The negative thoughts from that pesky inner critic is the story you tell yourself about yourself. That conversation is called self-talk and has a powerful influence on how you view yourself and the world around you.

Self-talk can be positive and compassionate. It might say kind things like, "You will get it next time" or "You are worthy of your dream" and encourage you to do hard things.

Self-talk can also be negative and unkind. It might say things like, "You will never be good enough" or "You are a failure" and stir up negative feelings.

Over time, these feelings will influence the way you view yourself and that will impact every part of your life.

When you have a low view of yourself it can cause you to feel anxious, to behave differently, and to perform poorly at school. However, when you have a positive view of yourself, you are more resilient, and more likely to overcome disappointment, failure, and obstacles. Additionally, you have richer relationships and achieve better grades.

A positive self-view is not about thinking you are amazing and perfect, it is about reframing hard things with a growth mindset, recognizing your potential, and the compassion to talk kindly to yourself.

Next time your inner critic starts yapping mean things about you do the following:

- **Identify the feelings behind the negative self-talk.**

    For example, when I was getting ready to rappel down the mountain, the negative things I was saying about myself were "I cannot," "There is no way I can do that," and "I am just not brave enough."

    What I was feeling though was fear. Being brave is not the absence of fear but overcoming fear.

- **Acknowledge and reframe your feelings.**

    Feeling fear is normal, especially when you are hanging 8,000 feet in the air by a thin rope. I do not know if you can fly, but I cannot. Additionally, it was the first time I ever went rock climbing. This was a new experience, and new things can be scary at first.

    There is no reason for me to think I am not brave enough. Fear, under these circumstances, is a perfectly natural and normal response.

- **Be kind to yourself.**

  As I stepped to the edge of the mountain, I remembered a quote by Athena Signh, "Never trust your fears, they do not know your strength."

  Facts.

  I reminded my inner critic that I can do hard things and things I never thought were possible; that I am courageous enough to face my fears and overcome them; and that I am brave enough to rappel down this mountain.

  And I did. I totally did it. I am brave.

  It was fun and an experience I will never forget. In fact, I want to do it again one day. I am glad I did not let fear rob me of this experience.

After acknowledging and reframing your negative thoughts, respond to yourself with compassion, kindness, and positive affirmation. Remind yourself that you can do hard things and things you never thought were possible.

What you say to yourself matters. It influences the way you view yourself and impacts your grades, goals, and mental health. Whenever your inner critic gets loud and mean make sure to identify, acknowledge and reframe your feelings, and respond to yourself with kindness.

DISCUSSION QUESTIONS

1. What is self-talk, and how does it influence our view of ourselves and the world around us?

2. How can negative self-talk affect our behavior and performance at school?

3. What are some examples of positive and negative self-talk, and how can we reframe negative self-talk into positive self-talk?

4. How can responding to negative self-talk with compassion and positive affirmation improve our mental health?

5. What steps can we take to change our negative self-talk into positive self-talk?

TALK TO YOURSELF LIKE YOU WOULD TO SOMEONE YOU LOVE.

BRENE BROWN

NOTES

"THE ONLY THING THAT WILL STOP YOU FROM FULFILLING YOUR DREAMS IS YOU."

TOM BRADLEY

EMOTING
THROUGH NEGATIVE SELF-TALK

NEAGTIVE SELF-TALK

POSITIVE AFFIRMATION

I'M NOT GOOD ENOUGH.

I'M ENOUGH & WORTHY OF MY DREAMS!

CHAPTER 6

I CAN.
I WILL.

"For anyone out there not sure they can do something. I am here to tell you that you can do it!"

— Rob Mendez

"Who says I can't? Nobody!"

Those are the closing words of an inspirational speech by Coach Rob Mendez as he accepts the Jimmy V Award for Perseverance at the 2019 ESPY Awards.

Mendez has no limbs. He has never thrown a football, run on a field, tackled or blocked anyone, yet he is the head coach of the Junior Varsity Football team at

Prospect High School.

You are probably thinking, "impossible!"

No, it is completely possible. In fact, during the 2018 school year coach Rob led his team to the league JV championship. He did so by riding up and down the football field on his motorized wheelchair, drawing up plays with his mouth, and inspiring his players to believe in themselves.

Rob Mendez was born with a rare congenital disorder called tetra-amelia syndrome that is characterized by the absence of arms and legs. As you can imagine, living without limbs presents all types of challenges, but Rob refuses to be defined by his limitations. His father taught him to embrace his differences, to push the limits and prove the doubters

wrong. But doing so was not easy.

Ever since Rob fell in love with football, a passion for coaching emerged. His dream was to be a head coach. But how can Rob possibly coach a game he is never physically played?

There was doubt.

While there are clearly some things that Rob cannot physically do, it is his determination over his limitations, and his belief of doing the impossible that drives Mendez to learn how to play the game of football.

It all started with a PlayStation. Rob taught himself the fundamentals of football by playing the Madden video game. He figured out how to use the controllers by pressing the buttons with his chin and collarbone. He studied the offensive and defensive schemes. Over time Rob developed a great football mind. In fact, Mendez came in second place in a 32-team Madden tournament organized by his high school friends.

During his freshman year, Rob decided to take his knowledge of the game to the field and became team manager of his high school's football team. At home he would draw up game plans on Madden and bring them to practice. By senior year Mendez was promoted to quarterbacks coach.

After graduation Rob continued to pursue his passion. He spent the next 12 years as an assistant coach at various high schools. In 2018, Rob's dream finally came true as he was named head coach of Prospect High School's Junior Varsity football team. That season he led the Prospect Panthers to an 8-2 record and a playoff berth.

Rob's story is nothing short of incredible. His perseverance is inspiring. His belief to achieve the

impossible has captivated the hearts of his players and is changing the football community.

At the Espy Awards Coach Mendez reminds the nation, "For anyone out there not sure they can do something. It can be in sports, it can be in your job, it can be in your lives. Whatever it is, I am here to tell you that you can do it."

YOU CAN DO IT

Here are a few things I learned from Jim Abbott's story:

- **Believe in yourself**: Coach Rob Mendez's story teaches us to believe in ourselves and our abilities. We should never let our limitations or doubts stop us from pursuing our dreams.

- **Perseverance**: Rob Mendez's journey is a great example of perseverance. Despite his physical limitations, he continued to pursue his passion for football and coaching.

- **Focus on what you can do**: Rob Mendez couldn't physically play football, but he focused on what he could do - learn the game, study strategies, and coach the game he loves.

- **Embrace your differences**: Rob Mendez's father taught him to embrace his differences and not be defined by his limitations. We should all learn to embrace our differences and celebrate diversity.

- **Inspire others**: Rob Mendez inspired his team to believe in themselves and achieve greatness. We can all be a positive influence on others and inspire them to reach their full potential.

Coach Rob Mendez's story teaches us that nothing is impossible if we believe in ourselves and persevere through challenges. We need to focus on our abilities rather than our limitations and have the courage to try new things. By having a growth mindset, we can learn from failures and setbacks, and use them as opportunities for growth. It is time for us to challenge our beliefs and push ourselves out of our comfort zones. Let us adopt a can-do attitude and take action towards achieving our goals, no matter how big or small they may be. Remember, as Coach Mendez said, "For anyone out there not sure they can do something. It can be in sports, it can be in your job, it can be in your lives. Whatever it is, I am here to tell you that you can do it."

DISCUSSION QUESTIONS

1. Who is Rob Mendez, and why is he an inspiration?
2. What is tetra-amelia syndrome, and how does it affect Rob Mendez?
3. How did Rob Mendez learn the fundamentals of football?
4. What was Rob Mendez's role on his high school football team, and how did he contribute to the team's success?
5. What is the message that Coach Mendez wants to share with people who doubt their abilities?

DO NOT LET WHAT YOU CANNOT DO INTERFERE WITH WHAT YOU CAN DO.

– COACH JOHN WOODEN –

 # NOTES

"OBSTACLES DON'T HAVE TO STOP YOU. IF YOU RUN INTO A WALL, DON'T TURN AROUND AND GIVE UP. FIGURE OUT HOW TO CLIMB IT, GO THROUGH IT, OR WORK AROUND IT."

MICHAEL JORDAN

OVERCOMING
THE IMPOSSIBLE

Describe an obstacle you recently faced.

How can you see this differently and what can you learn from it?

What hard things do you need to do to overcome this obstacle?

Who would encourage you to bounce back? What would they say?

CHAPTER 7

DARE TO DREAM

Our goals can only be reached through a vehicle of a plan, in which we must fervently believe, and upon which we must vigorously act. There is no other route to success.

– Pablo Picasso

Here we are, chapter ten and nearly at the end of my book. (Thanks for sticking around!) I hope our time together has inspired you to rise above your circumstances and chase your im.possible dream.

As for me, I never did. I never chased my dream of playing Major League Baseball for the New York Yankees. Probably because I was terrible at baseball. I played left bench for my little league team. I was so terrible that my team gave my mother a full refund since I never played.

While I was terrible at baseball, I did not play in the Major Leagues because I gave up on my dream well before learning to play the game. I felt defeated and stopped believing in myself. Focused on my limitations, I did not realize my potential and stopped chasing my im.possible dream.

Since then, I've been on a mission to help students like you realize that you are not defined by your limitations but by your unlimited potential. I don't want you to let what seems to be impossible get in the way of what is possible. In fact, impossible is spelled...

I'M POSSIBLE!

You are capable of doing im.possible things and things you never thought were possible.

The truth is your dream is within your reach. There is no obstacle you cannot overcome. You are braver than you believe, stronger than you seem, and smarter than you think. You can do hard things. And you are worthy of your dreams.

It took me a very long time to learn that. Eventually I

started believing in myself, then I started dreaming again. Now, I am living my dream as a Youth Motivational Speaker. I get to empower students like you at schools, camps, and conferences all over the United States to believe in themselves and chase the impossible.

Speaking of inspiration, here is a spoken word piece I wrote titled, Dare to Dream. I usually recite it at the end of my school assemblies. The words have inspired tens of thousands of students to rise above their circumstances and chase their im.possible dream. I hope it inspires you too.

I dare you to dream
Dream like Martin Luther King
Dream big and dare to fear no man
The skies the limit
Take flight and fly like
Michael "Air" Jordan

It is just another obstacle
Mind over impossibilities
make your dreams possible
Risk and reward
Choice over chance
Float like a butterfly and
sting like the champ

At a glance

Life is more than random chances
More than the grand sum
of your circumstances
But a fraction of who you are
A vision to behold, a star
Your life, a mission to
unfold like mars

Inspired to dream? I hope you are. But you cannot chase a dream without a plan. Katherine Paterson once said, "A dream without a plan is just a wish." Your dream, however, is no wish. It's possible–so let us talk about developing a game plan.

S.M.A.R.T. GOALS

Goals are the first step to chasing your dream and are incredible motivators. They encourage action, confidence, and belief. Goals build resilience and raise the level of performance. They help make the impossible possible.

S.M.A.R.T. goals are specific, actionable, and attainable. They are broken down to smaller achievable steps. When you write goals down with a date in mind you are more likely to achieve them in a timely fashion. Here is a framework that will help you set smart goals.

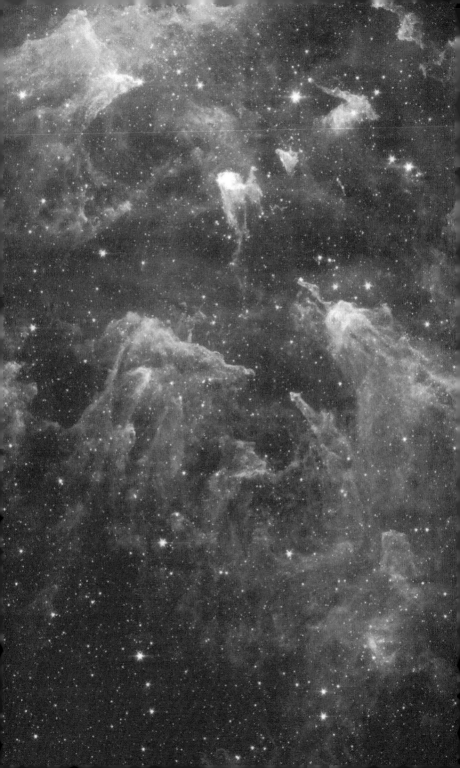

Specific. Smart goals are detailed, clear, and specific. They answer the questions, Who? What? Where? When? and How? Here is an example:

Goal: I want to get better grades in Math class.

S.M.A.R.T. Goal: I (who) want to get an A (what) in Math class (where) by the end of the marking period (when). I will study my notes for 30 minutes every night and meet with a tutor (how).

Measurable. Smart goals will help track your progress and determine when you have achieved them. They answer the questions, how much? How many? How well?

I want to get an A–is measurable. It will determine when you achieve your goal.

Attainable. Smart goals are actionable and challenging but realistically attainable. They answer the question, how will I accomplish the goal? Do I have the skills and resources to achieve them? Is the goal reasonably doable?

I will study my notes for 30 minutes every night and meet with a tutor–is actionable, challenging, realistic and describes how the goal will be accomplished.

Relevant. Smart goals are meaningful and draw you closer to realizing your dream. They answer the question, how will this goal help me achieve my dream?

I want to get an A in Math class–is relevant because you are a student. Additionally, an education will help you move closer to fulfilling your dream.

Time-bound. Smart goals are time based. They have a start and end date. They answer the question, what is the target date for accomplishing the goal?

By the end of the marking period–is time-bound and has a target date.

This S.M.A.R.T. Goal setting framework will help you develop a plan and empower you to do impossible things. Remember you cannot chase a dream without a plan. It is up to you to set the goals and work out the plan.

To help you do just that, I have created a IM.POSSIBL Goal planner using the S.M.A.R.T. goal setting method above. You can find the worksheets at the end of this chapter. Now that you have made it to the end of the book, go chase your dream. I dare you!

DISCUSSION QUESTIONS

1. What is the significance of having a plan in achieving success, according to Pablo Picasso?

2. How did the author learn to believe in himself and start dreaming again?

3. What is the S.M.A.R.T. goal-setting framework, and how can it help individuals achieve their dreams?

4. What is the importance of developing a plan in chasing one's dream?

5. How does goal setting help individuals build resilience and raise their level of performance?

A DREAM WITHOUT A PLAN IS JUST A WISH.

- Katherine Paterson -

GOAL PLANNER

EXAMPLE

▶ I DREAM OF

teaching math in high school

▶ LONG-TERM GOAL
Is it a personal goal? Is it realistic? Does it help me get closer to my dream?

I want to get an A in math class this school year

▶ THE BENEFIT
How will this goal help me achieve my dream?

It will help me learn math so that I can teach it one

day.

▶ WHO WILL HELP YOU WIN
Name a friend, teacher, coach who will help you achieve your goal when things get hard.

My tutor, parents and best friend.

▶ THE COST
What will I have to sacrifice in order to achieve my goal?

I will sacrifice my video game time to study.

▶ SHORT-TERM GOAL # ___1___

Action steps to achieve your long-term goal.

> Get an A in math class this marking period

▶ ACTION PLAN

This is the plan that will help you achieve your short-term goal.

I want to get an A in math class
(SHORT-TERM GOAL)

by 1 quater **so I will** study 30 mins everyday
(TARGET DATE) (ACTION STEP TO ACHIEVE YOUR GOAL)

and meet with my tutor **to achieve my goal.**

▶ PROGRESS

This is help you continue moving forward.

I will track my progress by monitoring my grades in class

after each text or quiz.

▶ STREAK

Check off a box every day that you complete your action step. Maintain a consecutive streak for 60 days and you'll establish a new habit.

☒	☒	☒	☒	☒	☒	☒	☒	☒	☒	☒	☒	☒	☒	☒	16	17	18	19	20
21	22	13	24	25	26	27	28	29	30	31	32	33	34	35	36	37	38	39	40
41	42	43	44	45	46	47	48	49	50	51	52	53	54	55	56	57	58	59	60

▶ REWARD

Write down a reward that will motivate you to achieve your goal. Once you do, get it.

my mother will treat me to ice cream

IM.POSSIBLE
GOAL PLANNER

▶ I DREAM OF

▶ LONG-TERM GOAL
Is it a personal goal? Is it realistic? Does it help me get closer to my dream?

▶ THE BENEFIT
How will this goal help me achieve my dream?

_____

_____

▶ WHO WILL HELP YOU WIN
Name a friend, teacher, coach who will help you achieve your goal when things get hard.

_____

_____

▶ THE COST
What will I have to sacrifice in order to achieve my goal?

_____

_____

▶ SHORT-TERM GOAL # _____
Action steps to achieve your long-term goal.

┌───┐
│   │
└───┘

▶ ACTION PLAN
This is the plan that will help you achieve your short-term goal.

I want to _____

_____
[SHORT-TERM GOAL]

by _____ **so I will** _____
[TARGET DATE]   [ACTION STEP TO ACHIEVE YOUR GOAL]

_____ **to achieve my goal.**

▶ PROGRESS
This is help you continue moving forward.

I will track my progress by _____

_____

_____

▶ STREAK
Check off a box every day that you complete your action step. Maintain a consecutive streak for 60 days and you'll establish a new habit.

1	2	3	4	5	6	7	8	9	10	11	12	13	14	15	16	17	18	19	20
21	22	23	24	25	26	27	28	29	30	31	32	33	34	35	36	37	38	39	40
41	42	43	44	45	46	47	48	49	50	51	52	53	54	55	56	57	58	59	60

▶ REWARD
Write down a reward that will motivate you to achieve your goal. Once you do, get it.

_____

_____

NOTES

"ALL OUR DREAMS CAN COME TRUE, IF WE HAVE THE COURAGE TO PURSUE THEM."

WALT DISNEY

NOTES

"BELIEVE YOU CAN AND YOU'RE HALFWAY THERE."

THEODORE ROOSEVELT

 # NOTES

"A DREAM DOESN'T BECOME REALITY THROUGH MAGIC; IT TAKES
SWEAT, DETERMINATION, AND HARD WORK."

COLIN POWELL

▶ NOTES

"THE BIGGEST ADVENTURE YOU CAN EVER TAKE IS TO LIVE THE LIFE OF YOUR DREAMS."

OPRAH WINFREY

THANK YOU

This is it. Our time together has come to an end. I just want to say thank you for reading my book. While challenging, I had a fun time writing this book for you. I was thinking about you every step of the way as I hoped to inspire you to rise above your circumstance, do hard things and chase your impossible dream. It turns out you've inspired me.

I've now achieved a dream that I thought was impossible, writing a book. But here I am, a published author.

If I can do that, imagine what you can do!

Did you ever finish reading the second chapter without blinking?

ABOUT THE AUTHOR

With over 20 years of experience in the youth market, school assembly speaker Eddie Cortes has been living out his life-long mission to empower students to build resilience and a positive self-worth.

This mission is personal for him. As a middle schooler, Eddie's dream of playing Major League Baseball for the New York Yankees came crashing down when his cousin told him that he was not big enough, fast enough, or talented enough to play pro ball. That moment crushed

Eddie's self-worth and he stopped chasing his dream.

From that point forward Eddie stopped believing in himself. In fact, his negative self-view impacted his grades, relationships, choices, and ultimately, he stopped dreaming.

This experience is what fuels Eddie's mission. He wants every elementary and middle school student to know that they are braver than they believe, stronger than they seem, smarter than they think, and worthy of their dreams.

Over the past several years Eddie has had the privilege to partner with public and private schools across the United States to share his message.

In his fun and interactive school assembly called IM.POSSIBLE, Eddie helps students to nurture a positive self-view and build resilience to overcome disappointment, failure, and obstacles.

His enthusiasm and passion are contagious. Eddie's ability to captivate elementary and middle school students with humor and storytelling draw students to the edge of their seats. His honest and thought-provoking approach will challenge every student to chase their dreams.

Eddie has a bachelor's degree in leadership, loves Chinese food, and is a CrossFit enthusiast. When he is not speaking, Eddie is making memories with his bride and daughter.

Follow Eddie Cortes on social:
- instagram.com/iameddiecortes
- facebook.com/youthspeakereddie
- linkedin.com/in/eddiecortes

To learn more about Eddie's school assembly, IM.**POSSIBLE**, visit:
- EddieCortes.com or
- email: info@eddiecortes.com or
- scan

51851965R00060